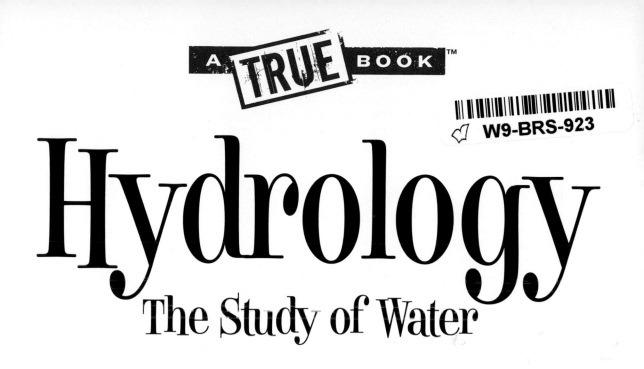

A TRUE BOOK™

Hydrology
The Study of Water

CHRISTINE TAYLOR-BUTLER

Children's Press®
An Imprint of Scholastic Inc.
New York   Toronto   London   Auckland   Sydney
Mexico City   New Delhi   Hong Kong
Danbury, Connecticut

Content Consultant
Jeffrey McDonnell, PhD
University Distinguished Professor of Hydrology
Director, Institute for Water and Watersheds
Richardson Chair in Watershed Science
Oregon State University
Corvallis, Oregon

Library of Congress Cataloging-in-Publication Data

Taylor-Butler, Christine.
  Hydrology the study of water/by Christine Taylor-Butler.
       p. cm.—(A true book)
  Includes bibliographical references and index.
  ISBN-13: 978-0-531-24677-1 (lib. bdg.)   ISBN-10: 0-531-24677-9 (lib. bdg.)
  ISBN-13: 978-0-531-28271-7 (pbk.)   ISBN-10: 0-531-28271-6 (pbk.)
  1. Hydrology—Juvenile literature. I. Title. II. Series.
  GB662.3.T393 2012
  551.48—dc23   2011030960

All rights reserved. Published in 2012 by Children's Press, an imprint of Scholastic Inc.
Printed in China 62
SCHOLASTIC, CHILDREN'S PRESS, A TRUE BOOK, and associated logos are trademarks and/or
registered trademarks of Scholastic Inc.
2 3 4 5 6 7 8 9 10 R 21 20 19 18 17 16 15 14 13 12

Find the Truth!

Everything you are about to read is true *except* for one of the sentences on this page.

Which one is **TRUE**?

T or F   Windmills were once used to control floodwater.

T or F   Hoover Dam is located in the Grand Canyon.

Find the answers in this book.

Contents

1 Water Everywhere

What is hydrology? 7

2 Hydrology in History

How did ancient civilizations affect how we
use water today? 13

THE BIG TRUTH!

Hoover Dam

How is the country's most powerful
river controlled? 20

Hailstones

3 The Hydrologic Cycle

How are climate and water
connected? 23

4

A Chinese rice paddy

4 Properties of Water

What are the three states of water? 31

5 Hydrology in Action

What are hydrologists doing to solve
Earth's problems? 37

True Statistics 43

Resources 44

Important Words 46

Index 47

About the Author 48

More than two
percent of Earth's
water is frozen.

5

Niagara Falls is located
on the border between the
United States and Canada.

CHAPTER 1

Water Everywhere

Water exists all around us. It is in the air, on the ground, and deep below the surface of Earth. We cook with it, play in it, and bathe with it. When you take a drink of water, do you ever wonder where it came from? Do you wonder why the water that gives us life can also destroy a city? Scientists ask these same questions.

Niagara Falls consists of three separate falls: the American, Bridal Veil, and Canadian Horseshoe Falls.

Hydrologists sometimes collect and analyze water samples.

The Study of Water

Hydrology is the study of water on Earth. Scientists study how water behaves when it is a liquid, a solid, or a gas. They conduct experiments to find out where water travels and where it is stored on and beneath Earth's surface. Scientists look for ways to use water to help people. They also look for ways to conserve it. Scientists who study water are called hydrologists.

Hydrologists collect a lot of data. For example, they measure rainfall and snowfall. They use their measurements to predict where the rainwater and melted snow will go. Too much rain can cause rivers to overflow. The water may flood farmlands and cities. Rain that flows downstream from the mountains or other places is called **runoff**. Hydrologists pay attention to runoff levels and help issue flood warnings. Then people have time to prepare for an emergency.

Flash floods happen when heavy rain drains quickly to low-lying areas.

Lake Mead formed when Hoover Dam was built to hold back the Colorado River.

Too little rain can cause a drought. Desert states such as Arizona and Nevada could not survive without a constant source of water. Hydrologists help design dams that back up large rivers and capture water. This water can then be stored in a storage area called a reservoir until it is needed in an area that has too little water.

Hydrologists teach communities in desert areas how to plant gardens that conserve water. They identify plants that require very little water to survive. Using these plants helps people use less water.

Hydrologists also help farmers water their crops through **irrigation**. They study how water moves over and through the ground. This helps hydrologists make sure that fertilizers and pesticides used on the crops don't flow into lakes and streams. This would harm wildlife.

Many farms could not produce enough food without irrigation.

More than 75 percent of all water used in the world is for irrigation.

The Grand Canal in China is the longest human-built waterway in the world.

CHAPTER 2

Hydrology in History

For thousands of years, hydrologists have looked for ways to control water. They knew that heavy rain or snowfall in one region could cause serious flooding in other areas downstream. They designed canals, **levees**, and **dikes** to protect towns and farmland. They built underground pipes to transfer water to cities. They used water to power machines. We still use many of these methods today.

Construction of the Grand Canal began in 486 BCE.

Waterwheels and Aqueducts

The Romans used aqueducts to bring water to cities. The first **aqueduct** was built in 321 BCE. Aqueducts use gravity to move water through the system. If the water needed to travel down through a valley and then uphill, engineers used **siphons**. The water traveled across the valley and up through a closed pipe. The weight of the water pushed the water through the pipe to almost the same height on the other side.

Roman aqueducts were inclined just enough for water to flow across them.

Water moves a waterwheel, which then moves machinery.

Civilizations as far back as the ancient Greeks learned how to harness the power of water to produce energy. Waterwheels used the power of moving water to turn machinery and grind wheat.

Modern scientists use this process to create renewable forms of energy. Falling water can create enough electricity to power cities hundreds of miles away.

Darcy invented the modern Pitot tube in the mid-1900s.

Important Discoveries

In the early 1800s, scientists began to understand that the rain falling from the sky began as water in the oceans. French engineer Henri-Philibert-Gaspard Darcy demonstrated how water flows through objects that seem solid, such as soil or porous (holey) rock. He knew that the same principles could be used to understand how water travels through the ground. Darcy invented the modern Pitot tube, a device used to measure water flow.

Floods: Friend or Foe?

Floods can sometimes be useful. Flood irrigation was first used in Egypt when the Nile overflowed each summer and fall. The flood waters carried fertile soil to farmland along the banks. Early hydrologists helped farmers plan crops around the wet and dry seasonal changes.

Floodwater is used in China to irrigate rice paddies. The roots of the rice plants grow best when covered with water.

Rice paddies that use irrigation provide 75 percent of the world's rice.

Rice grows only in very wet areas.

For more than 2,000 years, hydrologists and engineers in the Netherlands built dikes and canals to keep seawater from flooding towns. Windmills were used to pump water back to the sea. Today, electric pumps are used. In 1953, a storm raised the sea level several feet. More than 1,800 people were killed. Engineers designed better ways to control floods. Dutch dikes are now the strongest in the world.

Dikes have been built or strengthened in places such as Zeeland in the Netherlands.

New Orleans is about 6 feet (1.8 meters) below sea level.

Levees in New Orleans weren't designed for a hurricane as strong as Katrina.

When the Levees Failed

Levees can be built to protect towns located below sea level. On August 29, 2005, Hurricane Katrina hit New Orleans, Louisiana. The water did not flow over the levee. Instead, the force of the water moved the soil beneath the levees. The levees collapsed, and water flooded 80 percent of the city. The U.S. Army Corps of Engineers is building stronger levees using methods invented in Holland.

Hoover Dam

Hoover Dam is located on the Colorado River in the Black Canyon, near the Arizona-Nevada border. Construction crews worked for more than five years to build it. Before it was completed in 1936, land downstream was dry for most of the year. Each spring, the river swelled from snow melting in the Rocky Mountains. Hoover Dam controls seasonal flooding by holding water back until it is needed downstream.

Inside the dam, water is pumped through a system that creates electricity for Nevada, Arizona, and California.

Statistics:

- Completed in 1936
- 726 feet (221 m) tall
- 1,244 feet (379 m) long
- 660 feet (201 m) thick at the base
- 45 feet (14 m) thick at the top
- Contains 4.5 million cubic yards (3.4 million cubic meters) of concrete
- Creates 4 billion kilowatt-hours of electricity each year
- 883,000 gallons of water per second are pumped through pipes

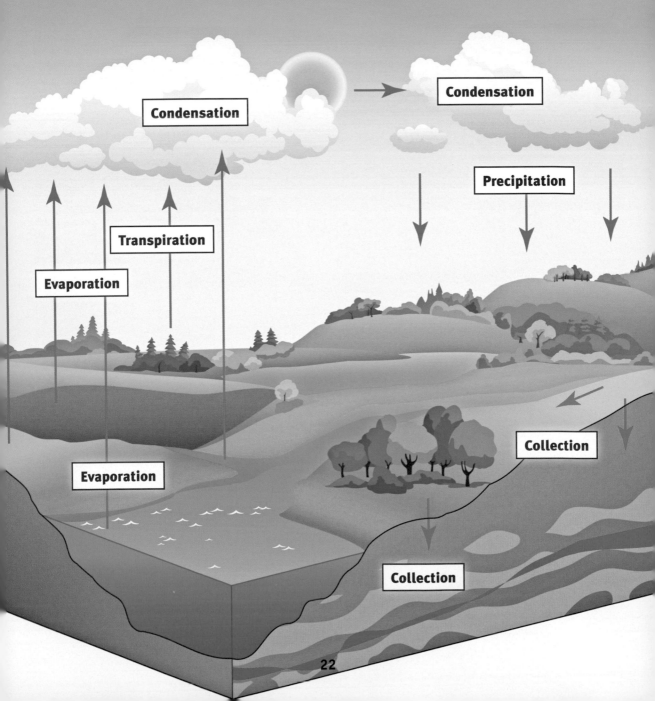

There is no beginning or end to the water cycle.

Condensation

Condensation

Precipitation

Transpiration

Evaporation

Collection

Evaporation

Collection

CHAPTER 3

The Hydrologic Cycle

All life on the planet depends on the water cycle. This process is also called the **hydrologic cycle**. This cycle is responsible for weather patterns and climate. Hydrologists study the cycle to look for changes in the pattern that might create emergencies or make water unsafe for humans and animals. The hydrologic cycle has no beginning or end.

The hydrologic cycle has five basic parts. They are evaporation, transpiration, condensation, precipitation, and collection.

Evaporation

Evaporation is the process when the energy from the Sun warms Earth's liquid water and turns it into water vapor in the air. Liquid water covers about 70 percent of Earth. It is in oceans, rivers, lakes, and other bodies of water. The soil also contains some water.

Evaporation and transpiration are related.

Water covers more than 70 percent of the planet's surface.

Plants use only a very small amount of the water they draw from the soil.

Roots give a plant stability.

Transpiration

Plants add to the water vapor in the air through transpiration. A plant draws water from the soil through its roots. The plant uses some of the water. The rest of the water evaporates through the leaves or needles.

All of this water vapor mixes with the air. This creates **humidity**. Humidity is a measure of how much water vapor is in the air.

Clouds are made from millions of tiny water drops.

Condensation

Warm air rises. Water vapor rises with it. As the air travels away from Earth, it cools. Cool air cannot hold as much humidity as warm air can. Eventually, the air reaches a temperature where water vapor turns into liquid droplets. This process is called condensation.

As more water vapor becomes liquid, the droplets gather into clouds.

Precipitation

Wind pushes the clouds to different locations on the planet. The water droplets continue to collect into bigger and heavier clouds. Soon, the droplets become heavy enough to fall back to Earth. This falling water is precipitation. It often falls as rain. In colder temperatures, precipitation might fall as snow, sleet, or hail.

Hailstones are chunks of icy precipitation.

Collection

Some precipitation falls directly into rivers, lakes, or oceans. Some falls on land. When precipitation falls on land, some of the water flows downhill, eventually collecting in rivers or lakes. Much of the water soaks into soil. Plants draw part of the water through their roots. The rest continues down into the ground to collect in **aquifers**. Whether the precipitation falls on water or land, the hydrologic cycle begins again.

A watershed is an area of land that drains water to a lower part of the landscape.

Finding Freshwater

Humans need freshwater to live. They cannot drink the saltwater of the oceans. But only about three percent of Earth's water is freshwater. Hydrologists study aquifers to look for freshwater sources. They study groundwater to find out if it is contaminated with pesticides or toxic materials. Hydrologists help cities design sewers to carry away water during storms. They design equipment to purify water that can be used for drinking.

Water is cleaned before it reaches your home.

CHAPTER 4

Properties of Water

A water molecule is made from two hydrogen atoms and one oxygen atom. The chemical formula for water is H_2O. H stands for hydrogen. O stands for oxygen.

Water is a unique substance. It is the only type of matter that naturally exists on Earth in three different states: liquid, solid, and gas.

← The U.S. Congress passed the Clean Water Act in 1972.

Water molecules can slide over one another. That is why liquid water takes the shape of any container it fills. When heat is applied, the molecules move farther apart. Eventually the bonds connecting water molecules to one another break. Water becomes a gas vapor when the temperature reaches 212 degrees Fahrenheit (100 degrees Celsius).

Timeline of Advances in Hydrology

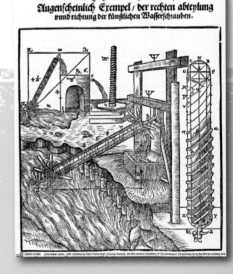

400 CE
The use of a rain gauge is first recorded in India.

4000 BCE
Ancient Egyptians create canals, dams, and levees.

1st century BCE
Marcus Vitruvius publishes detailed drawings of aqueducts and siphons.

When the temperature cools, water molecules slow down. If the temperature falls below 32°F (0°C), the water molecules lock in place and form solid ice. This is called the freezing point. When the temperature rises above the freezing point, the ice melts and becomes a liquid or vapor once again.

Water has an unusual property. Its volume expands when it freezes. Water can break a metal pipe if it is trapped inside when it freezes.

1920
The first tsunami warning system is developed to warn Hawaiians of coastal floods.

1732 CE
Henri Pitot creates the early Pitot tube to measure stream speed.

1879
The first hydroelectric dam in North America is built at Niagara Falls.

Pure water has no taste, color, or odor. The water in your glass, however, is not pure. It contains dissolved minerals and chemicals. Minerals get into the water when it filters through the ground. Chemicals are sometimes added to make the water safe for human use.

Seawater is also unpure. Salt is mixed in. Humans cannot survive on saltwater, but ocean creatures can. Some animals' bodies filter the salt out of the water. Others get the water they need from their food.

Ice floats on water because it contains air.

Hydrologists work to find new ways of conserving water.

Water is heavy. Gravity pulls water downhill until something gets in the way to stop it. When dropped from a tall height, water can drive a **turbine**.

Water is also a **solvent**. It can seep into porous objects and dissolve them. This is why some materials break down when exposed to water.

Hydrologists study these properties to design experiments. Their studies can lead to safer drinking water and better use of resources.

Boats called gondolas are a popular means of transportation with tourists in Venice, Italy.

CHAPTER 5

Hydrology in Action

Hydrology plays an important role in keeping the planet healthy. Hydrologists work with engineers and other scientists to design solutions to some of the world's problems. They find ways to create renewable sources of energy. They help design devices that alert the public to potential dangers when bad weather arrives. Hydrologists are even helping NASA study the frozen water on Mars. Hydrologists are constantly inventing new ways to control water.

← Venice, Italy, is built on 117 small islands.

The Sinking City

Venice, Italy, was built in a lagoon. A lagoon is a shallow body of water that is connected to the sea. Venice's buildings are sinking. The sea level is rising. In 1996, Venice flooded 100 times. The first floors of most buildings in Venice are no longer usable.

Hydrologists have developed a way to prevent more flooding. They designed gates that rise out of the water when a high tide approaches, blocking the water. The gates lower when the water level goes down.

Venice's flood-gate system helps to keep the city safe.

Underwater turbines are similar to windmills.

Underwater Windmills

In New York, hydrologists helped design underwater turbines that work much like windmills. The turbines spin below the East River when the tide flows toward the land. They spin again when the tide rolls back out to sea. This creates a source of clean, renewable energy. Scientists are studying the data to make sure fish are not harmed.

The Central Arizona Project Canal brings water from the Colorado River to the deserts of Arizona.

The Arizona Water Bank

Arizona receives a share of the water from the Colorado River. Because the state does not use its full amount, the government created a water bank. This guarantees that water is available to use in times of drought.

Some water is stored in an aquifer. The rest is used to irrigate crops so farmers do not have to pump water from underground.

Collecting Clean Water

Drought is a major problem in many African nations. In some places, people must walk several miles to collect water. The water is often used by wildlife and may be contaminated. Hydrologists use solutions created in other parts of the world to help solve this problem. Using towers or buckets to collect rain helps provide a cleaner source of water.

Collected rainwater can be carried to wherever it is needed.

41

Hydrologists are not afraid to get wet!

So You Want to Be a Hydrologist?

Hydrologists study math, geology, biology, and engineering in college. They use those skills to solve problems. They spend a lot of time outdoors. Hydrologists use gauges, flow meters, pumps, and many other scientific tools to collect and analyze water data.

If you want to be a hydrologist, be prepared to get wet! ★

True Statistics

Longest river in the world: Nile River, at 4,134 mi. (6,653 km)

Amount of water used in the United States each day: More than 400 billion gal. (1.5 trillion L)

Percentage of Earth's water that is freshwater: About 2.5 percent

Percentage of freshwater that is available for drinking: Less than 0.007 percent

Largest location of freshwater: Glaciers in Antarctica and Greenland

Largest ocean on Earth: Pacific Ocean

Smallest ocean on Earth: Arctic Ocean

Did you find the truth?

 Windmills were once used to control floodwater.

 Hoover Dam is located in the Grand Canyon.

Resources

Books

Higgins, Matt. *Clear Choices: The Water You Drink*. Chicago: Norwood House Press, 2011.

Just Add Water: Science Experiments You Can Sink, Squirt, Splash, Sail. New York: Children's Press, 2008.

Rice, William B. *Water Scientists*. Minneapolis: Compass Point Books, 2010.

Rosenberg, Pam. *Waterfall Watchers*. Chicago: Raintree, 2012.

Simon, Charnan, and Ariel Kazunas. *Super Cool Science Experiments: Water*. Ann Arbor, MI: Cherry Lake Publishing, 2010.

Sohn, Emily, and Erin Ash Sullivan. *Weather and the Water Cycle: Will It Rain?* Chicago: Norwood House Press, 2012.

Organizations and Web Sites

American Museum of Natural History
Water: H_2O = Life
www.amnh.org/exhibitions/water
Find fun facts about water, water cycles, and current projects going on around the world.

USGS—Water Science for Schools
http://ga.water.usgs.gov/edu/index.html
Learn about water sources, the water cycle, and research in action.

Places to Visit

Fairmount Water Works Interpretive Center
The Delaware River Basin's Watershed Education Center
640 Waterworks Drive
Philadelphia, PA 19130
(215) 685-0723
www.fairmountwaterworks.org
Enjoy interactive water activities, live fish cams, and a simulated helicopter ride.

Hoover Dam/Lake Mead Reservoir
Nevada Route 172
On Nevada/Arizona border
(866) 730-9097
www.usbr.gov/lc/hooverdam
Visit the dam, learn about hydroelectricity, and explore the reservoir.

 Visit this Scholastic web site for more information on hydrology:
www.factsfornow.scholastic.com

Important Words

aqueduct (AK-wuh-dukt) — a man-made channel for carrying water over valleys and rivers

aquifers (AK-wih-furz) — places beneath the ground where freshwater collects

dikes (DIKES) — high walls or dams that are built to hold back water and prevent flooding

humidity (hyoo-MID-i-tee) — the amount of moisture in the air

hydrologic cycle (hye-druh-LAH-jik SYE-kul) — the constant movement of Earth's water

irrigation (ir-i-GAY-shuhn) — the supplying of water to crops by man-made means

levees (LEV-eez) — banks built up near a river to prevent flooding

runoff (RUN-awf) — water that flows from a higher area to a lower one

siphons (SYE-fuhnz) — bent tubes through which liquid can drain upward and then down to a lower level

solvent (SAHL-vuhnt) — a substance, usually a liquid, that can make another substance dissolve

turbine (TUR-buhn) — an engine powered by water passing through the blades of a wheel and making it spin

Index

Page numbers in **bold** indicate illustrations

aqueducts, **14**, **32**
aquifers, 28, 29, 40

canals, **12**, 13, 18, 32, **40**
Central Arizona Project Canal, **40**
Clean Water Act (1972), 31
climate, 23
clouds, **26**, 27
collection, **22**, 23, **28**, **41**
Colorado River, **10**, 20, **40**
condensation, 22, 23, **26**
conservation, 8, 11, **35**

dams, **10**, **20–21**, 32, **33**
deserts, 10, 11, **40**
dikes, 13, **18**
drinking water, 29, **30**, 35
drought, 10, 40, 41

electricity, 15, 18, 20, 21, **33**, 37, 39
engineers, 14, 16, 18, 19, 37
evaporation, **22**, 23, 24, 25

farming, 9, **11**, 13, **17**, 40
flooding, **9**, 13, **17**, 18, **19**, 20, **33**, **38**

Grand Canal, **12**, 13
groundwater, 11, 16, 28, 29, 34

Hoover Dam, **10**, **20–21**
humidity, 25, 26
Hurricane Katrina, **19**
hydrologic cycle, **22**, 23, 28
hydrologists, **8**–9, 10, 11, 13, 17, 18, 23, **29**, **35**, 37, 38, 39, 41, **42**

ice, 33, **34**, 37
irrigation, **11**, **17**, 40, **41**

lakes, **10**, 11, 24, 28
levees, 13, **19**, 32

molecules, 31, 32, 33

New Orleans, Louisiana, **19**
Niagara Falls, **6**, 7, 33
Nile River, 17

oceans, 16, **24**, 28, 29, 34

pesticides, 11, 29
Pitot tubes, **16**, 33
plants, 11, 17, **25**, 28
precipitation, 9, 10, 13, 16, 20, 23, **27**, 28, 32, **41**

rain gauges, 32
reservoirs, **10**
rivers, 9, **10**, 17, 20, 24, 28, 39, **40**

saltwater, 29, 34
sea level, 18, 19, 38
siphons, 14, **32**
soil, 16, 17, 19, 24, **25**, 28
storms, 18, **26**, 29

temperatures, 26, 27, 32, 33
timeline, **32–33**
tools, **16**, 32, 33, 42
transpiration, **22**, 23, 24, 25
tsunamis, **33**

Venice, Italy, **36**, 37, **38**

warning systems, 9, 33, 37
water cycle. *See* hydrologic cycle.
water samples, **8**, **29**, **42**
watersheds, **28**
water vapor, 24, 25, 26, 32, 33
weather, 23, 37
wind, 27
windmills, 18, 39

About the Author

Christine Taylor-Butler is the author of more than 60 books for children, including the True Book series on American History/Government, Health and the Human Body, and Science Experiments. A graduate of MIT, Christine holds degrees in both in civil engineering and art and design. She currently lives in Kansas City, Missouri.